Change

OUR EVER-PRESENT COMPANION

Reflections
from the
Red Kayak

By **Mary Anne Smrz**

An NBCS, Inc. Production

Email: info@redkayakinstitute.org

Website: www.redkayakinstitute.org

Change, Our Ever-Present Companion: Reflections from the Red Kayak

Published in the United States by Pearl Editions, LLC.

Cover Design by Ann Moss

Photographs by Mary Anne Smrz, unless otherwise noted. Printed in the United States

ISBN: 0-9859123-8-3

ISBN-13: 978-0-9859123-8-3

The purpose of this book is to inspire and comfort. The information is designed to acquaint individuals with the process of journaling as a way to gain insight. Neither the author nor the publisher is engaged in rendering medical or counseling advice. If such advice is required, the services of a qualified medical professional should be sought. The author and publisher shall not be held liable or responsible to any person or entity with respect to any loss or damage caused or alleged to be caused, directly or indirectly by the information contained in this publication.

1. Diaries–Authorship. 2. Journals–Authorship. 3. Journal writing. 4. Kayaking 5. Nature journaling 6. Mind-body connections

For —

Embrace the change — joy and a beautiful gift of life! Keep Paddlin' on!

[signature]

To deebeckmann

"It all comes right on the water."

Other Books by Mary Anne Smrz:

Reflections from the Red Kayak: Thoughts on Life

A Season on the Water: Reflections from the Red Kayak

A Year of Transformation: Reflections from the Red Kayak (ebook only)

Table of Contents

Acknowledgements

First and most importantly, this book would not have come to completion without the love and support of Dee Beckmann to whom this book is dedicated. Your encouragement for my writing gave me the confidence to finish this book. Your generous gift of the Writer's Retreat in northern Wisconsin was priceless. Thank you for being such a beautiful companion on this journey of change. I could not have done any of it without you.

My journey of transition has been deeply enriched by my friendship with my business partner, Jason Dobrzynski. Jason, you and I have been on an incredible journey in our financial and life planning work at Waddell and Reed. We have shepherded each other through many unexpected shifts in our lives. We have walked a time of transition unlike any other, and we walked it beautifully together. Going forward into this new chapter of the practice, your clients' lives will continue to be enriched by your caring way and the level of trust and integrity you bring to everything you do. Our friendship is one of the most important relationships in my life.

To the other members of our Waddell and Reed team who walked this journey of transition with me, Maralynn Kearney, Lorelei Johnson and Natasha Russell, your unwavering belief in this process and your commitment to help every step of the way was invaluable.

Writing this book has taken me on an emotional journey back through my twenty-three-year career as a financial advisor. Friends who became clients, clients who became friends, co-workers unlike any other and a supportive company. How my life could be so blessed! There have been many changes in so many of your lives through the years, and I am honored to be a part of them. We walked some incredible paths together for which I am grateful. The gifts you gave me along the privileged journey of working with you are immeasurable.

The work of the Red Kayak Institute was a major influence on this book. Change: Our Ever-Present Companion was the theme of our retreats. To Dee Beckmann, Ann Moss, Josette Songco, Josette Szalko, Colleen Thomas—my Red Kayak Institute board, there are no words to express my deep gratitude for all you do and all you are. We shared many incredible retreat experiences and fabulous board meetings. Our retreaters' lives are better because of you and all you bring to every retreat. In the words of the Arcturians, "Your work is not to drag the world kicking and screaming. Your job is simply to do your work, sacredly, secretly and silently and those with eyes to see and ears to hear will respond." You do this so beautifully every time you so warmly welcome our retreaters, care for them when they are on the water, and share a part of yourselves with your insights. Thank you for helping so many reclaim themselves and receive the healing benefits of kayaking. Just add water.

To Sharon Kelleher and Linda Conley from the Edward Cancer Center in Naperville, Illinois. This year we celebrated our fifth retreat with you, and you were our first. Thank you for taking a chance on us and allowing us the sacred experience for both the cancer survivors and their caregivers to receive a small slice of healing on the water. The essay in this book, "The Shift," is the sweet story of our first retreat together.

To the Development Staff at Mother McAuley High School for entrusting us with the privilege of raising money for the Jan Malloy Memorial Scholarship by hosting a paddling retreat in her memory. She loved kayaking and her presence is with us as we share time with your faculty, staff and alumnae on the water. In the words of Catherine McAuley, your foundress, "No work of charity can be more productive or good to society than the careful instruction of women." We are honored to be able to help continue her mission of educating young women to serve the needs of others through Jan's scholarship. And to our scholarship recipient speakers and the A Cappella Choir from McAuley, you added so much to the retreat experience by sharing your gifts.

To all of the retreat participants in our Recovery on the Water series and all our retreaters, your input and helpful suggestions were invaluable in helping us shape the mission of the Red Kayak Institute. Our reciprocal sharing was amazing, and you will never know how many gifts you gave us and how you helped our institute grow.

To Sherrie and Joe Anicich from The Purple Project, their nonprofit organization which benefits parents who have lost children. Thank you for including us on your retreat program. To see the healing that occurred for these parents was incredible as they continue to navigate the uncharted waters of their unimaginable grief. Thank you for paddling with us.

Our work at the Red Kayak Institute could not be possible without the financial support of our many donors and those of you who came out on rainy mornings to support us in the DuPage Human Race 5k Run. Also, to Gerri Crane, from whose foundation, *The Friendship Fund* in Boston, we received our first grant and Janine and Bob McDonald who supported us with a grant through *The Ayco Foundation*. Thank you for believing in us and our mission.

I am grateful to the Lucafo family, Anthony, Laura, Vince and Annelise, for always supporting RKI in unexpected and thoughtful ways. You are so dear to my heart. And to Joanne and Ken Steichmann for the "full rental" of your boats for our retreats.

Although it sounds strange, I also want to express gratitude for my old Hyundai Veracruz and my new Hyundai Santa Fe, "Big Red," that safely carried our Red Kayak Institute trailer, *Clickety Clack*, loaded with boats to many retreats. Special thanks to my dear friend, Mary Kay Walsh, for her help in buying "Big Red." What a fun-filled day we shared.

I am also thankful for the Saganashkee Slough, the home base of our retreats. Magical things happened on those waters for our retreaters.

The Marywood Franciscan Spirituality Center in northern Wisconsin was the peaceful and contemplative haven for the final completion of this book. To Sr. Julia, for facilitating a fabulous Writer's Retreat. To Sr. Marla, Sr. Anita, and Deb our awesome cook from the Red Cliff Indian Reservation in Bayfield, Wisconsin, you were so much a part of the experience. And to my fellow writers with whom I shared so much – Juliet, Wendie, Mollie, Tom, Kaye, Rilla, and Deb – may your words continue to inspire and touch many lives in the years to come. It was an honor to be in your presence.

To Joan Anderson, the constant and unwavering compass of your inspiration continues to guide me. You affirm me in a way that is rare in my life, and your continued encouragement of my writing buoys me as I journey. I am ever grateful for the reciprocity of our friendship.

As always, this book would not be possible without the expertise of my editor, publisher and dear friend Georgiann Baldino. Your steady guidance continues to help me navigate the course of my writing and I look forward to our continued collaborations in the years to come.

To Ann Moss, for creativity unlike any other, thank you for the cover design and your beautiful insights. I treasure the constant, refreshing honesty of our friendship. It brings a clarity to my life that I could never articulate to you, but is invaluable.

A special thanks to my treasured neighbor and fellow water lover, Karen Gebner, for the final proof reading and correcting a few typos. I love the story of you reading the water lily section and your son, Keith, calling to tell you he bought a kayak. Serendipity is a beautiful gift we share.

And finally, to my yellow lab, Bayfield. Still going strong after fourteen years, our journey together continues in amazing ways. I will always treasure our visit to your namesake town of Bayfield, Wisconsin. Along with change, you are my ever-present companion. Thank you for your loyalty and your unconditional love.

Mary Anne Smrz, November 2017

Between the completion of the writing of this book and the publish date, Bayfield peacefully crossed over the waters on the Rainbow Bridge, transitioning to her new life. Our relationship has now changed, and she and I will find new ways to communicate. Although her passing has unmoored me, she will always remain tethered to my heart. She is, and always will be, my ever-present companion, her paw print on my soul. Bayfield's story is the closing essay of this book. So poignant for change, our ever-present companion.

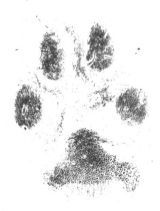

"The seas are the heart's blood of the earth. Plucked up and kneaded by the sun and the moon, the tides are systole and diastole of earth's veins."

—*The Outermost House: A Year of Life on the Great Beach of Cape Cod,* Henry Beston

Prologue

"Don't be afraid to take big steps. You can't cross a chasm in two small jumps."
—David Lloyd George

The opening quote for this book from *The Outermost House*, by Henry Beston is a favorite of mine, for each time I read it, I am graced with a new insight. The words are as fluid and flowing as their meaning. His reference to the sea and the tides "plucked up by the sun and the moon" reinforce for me the inner knowing that all of life is constantly changing. "Systole and diastole of earth's veins" are like our very own heartbeat.

In 1925, Henry Beston bought 50 acres of dune land on a barrier beach on Cape Cod and built a two room cottage. He always intended to use it as a vacation retreat. In September of the following year, he went there with the intention of staying for two weeks, but when it came time to leave, he could not go. In his own words, "the beauty and mystery of this earth and outer sea so possessed me and held me that I could not go." And there he spent the next year of his life.

In the introduction he wrote for the book, Robert Finch says this of Beston's writings: "As individuals, we have become far removed from direct participation in the patterns and particularities of the changing seasons. Insulated, air-conditioned, and jet-propelled, we have come to believe that we are largely independent of the earth's basic rhythms. Beston's unique strength as a nature writer lies in his ability to reconnect us emotionally and imaginatively to the primal, natural sources of our being, to link us to a world larger and more enduring than what he calls "our fantastic civilization." The importance and the lasting appeal of *The Outermost House*, I believe, is its power to remind us of how much, in our computer age, we still rely so much on the earth's deep constant rhythms, its basic integrity and equanimity."

I was first introduced to *The Outermost House* a few years ago on a trip to Cape Cod to visit my dear friend and author, Joan Anderson. She, too, retreated for a year, and her story is chronicled in her New York Times best-selling memoir, *A Year by the Sea*, which is now a motion picture. It is the narrative of the strength of a woman, stepping away to reclaim herself, and a story of profound change. Millions of lives have been enlightened and transformed by Joan's journey of self-discovery.

Both retreated for different reasons. Beston, because he felt a primal connection to the earth and the ocean. Anderson, because she knew she needed time away to sort out the next steps on her journey. Both felt an inner calling from the sea. Both were changed by their experience. Both allowed the shifts, transitions and transformations to slowly emerge over the course of their year at the water's edge.

Beston, referred to the shore as a place of constant change, never complete. Anderson, recognized that she is as unfinished as the shoreline along the beach. Change. Incompleteness. Unfinished. Their story. Our story. As universal as the "systole and diastole" of our hearts, our passions, our lives.

Change, Our Ever-Present Companion, this third book in the *Reflections from the Red Kayak* series, is a collection of essays of my own journey of change. Beginning in 2013 with a retreat I co-facilitated with Anderson on the shores of Trout Lake in northern Wisconsin; to attending one of her retreats on a trek to Iona, Scotland; to founding our nonprofit organization, the Red Kayak Institute; to transitioning out of my twenty-three-year career as a financial planner; and most importantly, to finding love, joy and contentment in my life, it has been a time of huge transformation. Unexpected and more beautiful than I could have imagined, I am truly following the mantra I came home from Iona with: **Trust the journey**.

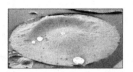

Your Droplets of Awareness...

Mollie's Miracle

"Miracles happen every day. Change your perception of what a miracle is and you'll see them all around you."
—Jon Bon Jovi

As we gathered for our daily lunch, Mollie came in with an announcement. "I have something to share with all of you," she proclaimed. While we enjoyed our meal, Mollie began her story.

"Since I was eleven, I have had problems with my left shoulder. In recent years, it has become more troublesome, and I was scheduled for shoulder replacement surgery next month." She paused and continued, "Yesterday we kayaked on Trout Lake. Heading out, I thought I would only paddle about 100 or 200 feet. But everyone was paddling to nearby Miller Island, and I decided to go with the group."

As Mollie spoke, I reflected back to the previous day on the water. The conditions were manageable when we left shore—a slight northwest breeze behind us as we kayaked to the island, blue skies and bright sunshine. After a pause for drifting and contemplation in the small cove by the island, we began paddling back.

In that short time in the cove, the wind increased considerably and the water became very choppy producing whitecaps in the distance. Mollie was paddling slowly but with a quiet determination.

"I used to be a biker," Mollie reflected. "I know what it takes to dig down deep to finish as you are nearing the end of a ride. I felt the same way out on the water."

I thought about paddling back with her, and along with the resolve on her face, I saw something else. A peacefulness. She was not stressed. She knew she would make it back in her own time. One stroke at a time.

Mollie continued. "When I came back from kayaking, I was achy and took a holistic remedy and then later an Aleve®. For the first time in a very long time, I was able to sleep on my left side and when I woke up, my pain and discomfort were gone. I called and cancelled my surgery."

I was stunned. For all of the snippets of emotional healing I have personally experienced and witnessed in others, I have never heard a story of physical healing. For her tenacity on the water, Mollie received a beautiful gift, a miracle actually. I have often read that a sense of inner peace, like I observed on Mollie's face, can bring about miracles.

Mollie is an Episcopalian priest and in the short time with her a profound faith was evident. As Marianne Williamson says in her book, *The Gift of Change*, "Faith means we're open to the possibility of miracles."

I have been in touch with Mollie since, and she unfortunately rescheduled her surgery. Was it still a miracle? Yes! She enjoyed a period of pain free relief and recognized that paddling helped her range of motion and bolstered forgotten shoulder muscles. Her spiritual belief, I think, was strengthened also.

Sometimes when you begin a book, you never know where the path takes you. Not necessarily the words on the page, but the experiences that accompany a creative project on its journey.

This publication is a collection of many reflections I wrote during the Red Kayak Institute retreat season. Our theme for the year, Change: Our Ever-Present Companion is the title of this book.

The Red Kayak Institute was born from the unexpected emotional healing that graced me from kayaking and continued with my writing. I thought, if paddling could be this healing for me, certainly others could benefit. Our mission for the institute is: *Encouraging people facing challenges to reclaim themselves and receive the healing benefits of kayaking. Just add water.*

Throughout the last five years, we have taken many people facing challenges on the water for half day and full day retreats – cancer survivors and their caregivers, women in recovery programs for addiction, parents who have lost children and "ordinary" people like you and me, not defined by any disease or life altering event.

When the group comes off the water, we do a circle of sharing about their experience. Time and time again, I hear that a small slice of healing occurred while on the water. Is it the simplicity of the kayak? Is it the paddling in silence? Is it the water itself? Or is it the combination of all three?

Listening to their stories, one of these three elements is more prominent, but the combination is the magic. Giving people permission to pause from hectic lifestyles to just "be" allows unresolved and percolating issues to surface. A sliver of emotional healing occurs, and in many cases, this repair allows for a change in course for that person.

As I complete this book, I am at the Marywood Franciscan Spirituality Center in the northwoods of Wisconsin on the shores of Trout Lake. In addition to our writing time, optional activities such as hiking and kayaking are available to us.

Since kayaking was involved, I offered Sr. Julia, the facilitator of the retreat, the opportunity to take a group out on the water for "Red Kayak Institute Lite," a scaled down version of our retreat format. Being back on Trout Lake became serendipitous for me. A little over four years ago, I assisted author Joan Anderson with her retreat on this lake and paddling here again brought back many fond memories. It was magical then and magical now.

For me, a recognition of oneness surfaced. In as much as my writing led to founding the Red Kayak Institute, the institute work enhances my writing. On many levels they become one. Each molds and shapes the other and I am just the conduit in the middle. I am grateful and humbled.

The cover of this book is an evergreen tree that greets me every time I paddle a certain stretch of the Manitowish River in Wisconsin. I was surprised at its transformation to a yellowish color in the fall. Change.

I purposely positioned the front of my kayak at the tip of the reflection of the tree. To me, it represents a connection to all things earthly and all things eternal. The shapes are the same, the front of the boat and the tree. Oneness.

One of my favorite quotes by Mahatma Gandhi is "be the change you want to see in the world." There are many turning points in our lives which evoke choices. Our lives are always evolving, with change as our ever-present companion. Choose wisely. Choose gratitude. Choose love.

Do you believe in miracles?

With inner peace, amazing gifts flow our way. How can you prepare yourself for the abundance that awaits?

Choose gratitude today. It will open your heart to miracles.

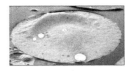

Your Droplets of Awareness...

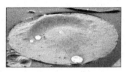

Your Droplets of Awareness...

The Zen of Preparation

*"The price of anything is the amount
of life you exchange for it."
—Henry David Thoreau, Walden*

One of my favorite Zen sayings is, "Chop wood. Carry water." These four simple words refer to the simplicity of everyday tasks, and the benefits of working through those seemingly mundane undertakings with mindfulness.

Almost as much as being on the water in my kayak, I love the preparation for a new season. Pulling the Red Kayak Institute's trailer, *Clickety Clack*, out of the garage and inspecting her for boat hauling duties fills my soul with the excitement of upcoming paddling adventures. There is much to do, and this year I decided to work through my anticipation being present to the task at hand slowly and mindfully.

To get ready for our season, I awaken the boats from their winter slumber, clean the exterior and vacuum the interior. Peering inside the boats, I find remnants of last year's season – sand, dry leaves, brittle twigs and Dark Chocolate Peanut Butter Kind® bar wrappers. I put duct tape on a few cracks in the seats and I smile at the precious memories of my time kayaking last year – with retreaters who participated with the Institute, sharing their thoughts and insights from being on the water, fun times with friends and a few fabulous solo paddles. I think of everyone who was able to reclaim a bit of themselves by experiencing the healing benefits of being on the water. The memories fill me with a sense of gratitude.

As I scrub out old coffee stains and apply this year's coat of UV Tech™ protection, I realize that I am also preparing myself, by opening my heart for the wonders to be received on the water this new season. Like with the kayaks, I scrub off the old outlived parts of my life and vacuum out the dust of what no longer serves me to make way for the unlived.

Getting ready for this paddling season, I find myself craving the unknown. Whenever I embark on a journey, be it an inward or outward voyage, the only thing I know for sure is that I will be different when it's over. Sometimes, we as humans, always want to know the outcome before we start. To realize we will be changed in the process is often a frightening concept. For isn't there security in things remaining the same? I think not. In fact I know not. What we think of as security are really things that keep us stuck when the real assurance is that all of life is moving, flowing, growing and changing.

Our preparation for these changes is as important as the trip itself. Often we rush through this step to get to the actual event. Today I discover peacefulness in the process and realize that attentiveness to the pacing of things can calm my spirit almost as much as being on the water. *Almost. Maybe. Well, not really.*

I recently read a quote by C. JoyBell C. that said, "I have come to accept the feeling of not knowing where I am going. And I have trained myself to love it. Because it is only when we are suspended in mid-air with no landing in sight, that we force our wings to unravel and alas begin our flight. And as we fly, we still may not know where we are going to. But the miracle is in the unfolding of the wings. You may not know where you're going, but you know that so long as you spread your wings, the winds will carry you."

To me, that quote is the essence of why being ready is so critical. A big part of preparation is letting go, sort of a "spring cleaning" of the soul. I recently read a list of things entitled *10 to Zen* that I want to share with you:

1. Let go of complaining
2. Let go of competing
3. Let go of judgments
4. Let go of anger
5. Let go of regrets
6. Let go of worrying
7. Let go of blame
8. Let go of guilt
9. Let go of fear
10. Have a proper belly laugh every day, especially if it's about your inability to let go of any or all of the above.

I finish cleaning the boats and load these sacred vessels on *Clickety Clack* and step back to see how beautiful she looks with eight boats ready for our first paddle of the Recovery on the Water series. She is ready to go, and so am I.

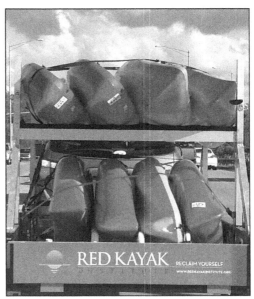

Photo by Josette Szalko

My new favorite Zen saying, "Haul boats. Paddlin' on.™"

At every step of our lives we are preparing for something. What is formulating for you now? Is it a big step in your life, or something small yet necessary?

Have you been able to really spend some time pondering what you are getting ready for and how that will affect your next steps?

How can you approach this action in a mindful way that will bring peace and calm to your process?

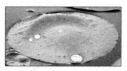

Your Droplets of Awareness...

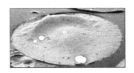

Your Droplets of Awareness

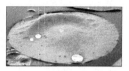

Your Droplets of Awareness...

We All Begin Somewhere

*"The only time you should ever look back
is to see how far you've come."*

-Anonymous

Sometimes it helps to look back before moving forward. Looking at our own personal history and ancestry gives us an understanding of what makes us who we are today. Often, gaining this perspective aids us to move through our own lives with more ease and clarity.

Dr. Henry Cloud, in his book, *Never Go Back*, shares 10 doorways to success on our journeys and how once we walk new paths, we never go back again. His message triggers memories of a very significant person in my life.

On November 1, 1893, a very special event occurred in my life, even though I wasn't yet a gleam in my parents' eyes. My maternal grandmother, Mary, was born in a small little farming town in Poland. She had a hard life and her family struggled to get by.

In December of 1913, my twenty-year-old grandmother bravely boarded the *Kaiser Wilhelm* ship, and headed across uncharted waters to begin a new chapter of her life, filled with new possibilities and opportunities in America. Amazing to think of her courage to make that decision and take that voyage.

I recently went to Ellis Island, where so many immigrants came through to America and found my grandmother's manifest. While reading the document, I could feel her there with me, hugging me into her. She came across in steerage, which is the lower deck of a ship where the cargo is stored. Steamship steerage decks were used to provide the lowest cost and lowest class of travel for immigrants to North America. The manifest indicated she was sponsored by her brother, John, who lived in Chicago.

One time, I asked her how she felt coming to America. She said she was terrified because everyone got examined for diseases and her papers were scrutinized. The tiniest mistake on her papers could send her back to Poland. Once she got through Ellis Island people were standing with signs bearing the destination cities—New York, Chicago, Philadelphia—and she just got behind the Chicago sign to the train that took her to her brother, John. Talk about trusting the journey!

My grandmother built a beautiful life in Chicago despite being very poor. All the immigrants struggled together, living in their ethnic neighborhood pockets. She and my grandfather raised four wonderful children, eventually owned their own home, worked tirelessly and created lasting friendships.

When she was 99, I interviewed her for a family video of her history. When I asked her how she felt about leaving Poland knowing she would never see her mother again, she quietly said in her sweet broken English, "You want a better life. You go to America. That's all." She never looked back and never went back. It was just that simple for her.

What does this story have to do with kayaking? For me, there are three lessons here.

First, she got in a boat. Although it was a little bigger than a kayak, she got in, knowing her life would never be the same again when she stepped off that ship. I feel that way every time I leave shore in my kayak and have witnessed this transformation in the paddlers who attend our retreats with the Red Kayak Institute. Something shifts, insights surface. We let go of things that no longer serve us. We come back to shore different than when we left. Small but significant changes emerge.

Second, she brought little. I have her two-by-three-foot steamer trunk she brought to America. In it was everything she owned. Imagine us trying to shove all of our stuff into something that size! Such is the same in a kayak. The tiny cockpit limits how much to take along. What do you take? Only the essentials, which is what I know my grandmother brought over. Every time I look at that trunk and every time I paddle, I am reminded of how little I need. The question that continually nudges me forward is, "How can I move easily and fluidly through life weighed down by so much material stuff?" My ancestors didn't need much and it's a good lesson for me. Perhaps it's why they were able to embrace change so easily because there was not much to let go of or to take along. The simplicity of my kayak reminds me of the refreshing concept of essentialism every time I paddle.

Third, knowing my grandmother's story, her strength, her courage and her willingness to embrace change reminds me to be strong in times of adversity in my life. When I think of long-ago changes that seem so hard, I reflect on her journey and gain perspective. Just like being on the water where weather conditions can shift abruptly and the scenery is different throughout the seasons, change IS our ever-present companion. The challenge is to welcome it with as much gusto as our ancestors.

My grandmother died on June 22, 1995 at the beautiful age of 101. I am honored to carry her name and she will always be an inspiration to me. I think America was good to her.

What is your history and how does it connect with you today?

How can your ancestors help you now with changes that are occurring in your life?

Is there one thing you can let go of to lighten your load today, and is there one thing you would put in your "steamer trunk" to take with you?

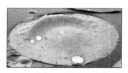

Your Droplets of Awareness...

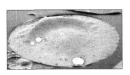

Your Droplets of Awareness...

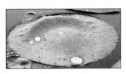

Your Droplets of Awareness...

From Winter to Spring, a Prolonged Transformation

"Sometimes our enthusiasm for change depends on our willingness to take a chance on tomorrow by risking what we have today."
—Courage to Change:
One Day at a Time in Al-Anon II

My faithful red kayak is patiently waiting for the slow shift from winter to spring. For the last 22 years, we have taken our first solo paddle together, and this year is no different. Except that we are waiting longer as Mother Nature takes her time with this drawn out change of season. I have decided that today is the day for the first solo paddle. The conditions are not necessarily ideal, but in the distance the open water calls to me, like a life-long friend anxious to be reunited once again. About 200 yards of ice and snow separate me from my friend, the water, and I first walk out with my paddle to tap it and test its thickness. Although there are some dark grey areas, which indicate slushier conditions, I find a path of solid ice that leads me to the water.

As I retrace my steps back to shore to get my kayak, I think about these less than perfect conditions for my first journey and winter's conversion to spring. In many times of our lives, transformation often occurs at times that seem less than ideal. We often want to wait until the we think situations are perfect or the time is right to make a change, and yet often, the best opportunities come at odd times when the circumstances seem less than optimal. Can you remember a time in your life when you knew it was time for something to shift, but it just didn't feel like the right time? I sure can. Sometimes I held back and sometimes I went ahead anyway, trusting that the timing would serve me. Grabbing my kayak and hauling it back across the ice, I recall this quote by Angel Chernoff, "Do not wait until the conditions are perfect to begin. Beginning makes the conditions perfect." So I begin.

I prepare to launch, and set my kayak next to a large, exposed tree trunk at the edge of the slushy ice.

The water is only inches deep here and I may need the help of the tree trunk to push myself off. Although it is only 47 degrees this morning, the blue sky reflecting off the water gives me a warm, comfortable feeling. I climb in my boat and give her a few nudges off the ice, past the tree trunk and out onto the water. *Ahhhh*, freedom. That ever present feeling for me every time I get in my kayak always seems more prevalent on the first paddle of the season.

The water levels on the lake are very low, purposely kept that way until a few weeks from now, when the dams are opened to let the spring runoff from northern Wisconsin work its way down the Wisconsin River. Soon, what I see out on the lake now—fields of deadheads and exposed sandbars—will be transformed and covered with water. This is a treat to be able to paddle over to these soon to be concealed elements. The lake is refreshingly unfamiliar as I head across to explore.

These fields of deadheads, which are the remaining trunks of trees which once stood here, have also been altered. Once tall pines and maple trees, these stumps now spend most of their lives under water. Visible at this time of year, they provide a temporary resting place for the Canadian geese and Mallard ducks that meander here. These trees have yielded their great stature, no longer have leaves to shed or branches to house birds, yet they still participate in the changing seasons. Peeking out above the water line, though different, they quietly make their presence known.

In our lives, too, we have experienced change like this. Things, people, and places that once were very prominent or important have become distant in their significance. Yet, their quiet essence still resonates somewhere in our memory, perhaps appearing momentarily now and then, to remind us of their subtle presence. Just under the surface, like the deadheads soon will be.

I paddle on farther and pull up on the shore of one of the open sandbars, which will soon be submerged in the transition to spring.

I feel as though I am kayaking on a new lake as I explore these unseen areas. The bare, moist brown sand has a different smell, like the ocean, and I smile as I observe a few seagulls flying overhead. The grains of sand on these little beaches will soon become the bottom of the lake and I am deep in thought of this seasonal rearranging of nature's gifts.

We often say the seasons change, but change seems more abrupt and faster than transformation. Just the length of the word has slowness about it. And sometimes in our lives, shifts occur gradually. Transformation begins from deep within and challenges us to trust the unknown, flowing slowly through us until it completely embraces us and we can take the next step. I close my eyes momentarily, inhale the "almost salty" smelling scent from the sand, listen to the waves gently lapping on this temporary shoreline and think of times of transition in my life. Times when I was experiencing an inner shift, yet not really mindful of it. Then, all of a sudden, something externally was different, and I come to the realization that all along I was processing a deep, life-altering sense of self-renewal.

I think one of our greatest challenges is to stop and sit quietly long enough to recognize, appreciate and embrace these gradual, transformational periods of our lives. Just as it is necessary for winter to turn to spring so life can begin anew, so it is important for continual alterations to occur on our journeys. We shed the old, outlived patterns to become something different.

I take my red kayak farther down the lake to a point of solid ice and turn around. I paddle back along the shore and am mesmerized by a huge blanket of ice and snow hovering over the shore. I would share a picture with you, but my camera battery died. (or changed?) So here is a rudimentary drawing:

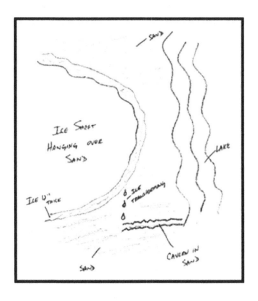

I am fascinated by the slow, deliberate melting of the ice. I sit here for a long time and watch this miraculous process, taking place moment by moment. Henry David Thoreau said in *Walden,* "All change is a miracle to contemplate, but it is a miracle which is taking place every instant." I feel I am witnessing a miracle, watching each little piece of hard ice turning into soft droplets of water and then the soft droplets strong enough to carve a mini cavern in the damp sand, each watery bead then joining the others in the lake. I am present to a natural cycle of evolution.

I, too, am one tiny drop in the sea of humanity, changing and becoming at my own pace, yet in rhythm with something larger than myself. I feel very insignificant, yet reassured that my transformation is part of a greater purpose. If we stop and think about it, we are all part of this bigger journey and each of us is participating on a small scale within the swirls and changes of our daily lives.

Do you find yourself in a period of transformation? Is it subtle or very dominant?

How does this change make you feel? Is it unsettling or do you feel "in the flow" entering a new phase of your life?

Right now, close your eyes, take a deep breath and envision this shift. Does it feel "right?" Will you embrace it or will you push it away?

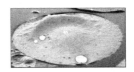

Your Droplets of Awareness...

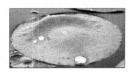

Your Droplets of Awareness...

Paddlin' on...and then again...

"All beginnings are somewhat strange, but
we must have patience, and little by little
we shall find things, which at first
were obscure, becoming clear."
—Vincent De Paul

My yellow lab, Bayfield, and I are on a Wisconsin odyssey to the northwoods during the first week of May. It is my intention to get out paddling on Trout Lake in preparation for the retreat I am assisting author Joan Anderson with later this month. But Mother Nature, as she often does, has other plans. Winter's stronghold on the lake is still evident at the icy shore.

Although I could see open water in the distance, there was no way to get there. From the frozen shoreline the water stretched out like one giant bowl of slush, like a Slurpee® from a 7-Eleven store. And not a mango orange or a pink strawberry, but a murky color to match the grayness of the day. When my friend Kit from the northwoods sent a late April picture of a "snowpaddler" (a snowman with a paddle,) I was shocked at how much snow was on the ground, but I figured by early May the water would be open, and I could get my little red vessel in for a spin around the lake.

Photo by Kit Bogenschneider

Instead, I stood on the beach and sighed and said to myself, "Ah, yet another test of patience." Patience is not one of my strongest virtues. I like to start at step one, move to step two and then leapfrog to step 10. The tediousness of going through steps three through nine makes me crazy. How often, in the busyness of our lives, do we jump forward trying to accomplish so much? I wonder what we really miss in the process.

I am really trying to learn calm endurance to appreciate the beauty in all the steps instead of focusing on the destination. And really, aren't we always "arriving?" Is there really a "destination" or is each new ending just a new beginning of something else? I think things can work much better for us if we are not always in such a hurry. If we can really slow down enough to appreciate all of life's miracles every day. All the steps.

I once read this saying, "Patience attains all it strives for." I look down at my normally high-spirited dog, Bayfield, as she calmly sits near me. I think she is just sitting there watching the ice melt.

I look out at the lake with her and sure enough, I can see patches of slushy ice slowly disappearing and I think to myself, this is the gift of this day. To witness the "arrival" of water. To appreciate this gift of nature, however slowly it unfolds. And for today, patience unexpectedly wins me over. I sit down next to Bayfield and together, for a long while, we watch the ice melt.

Photo by Dee Beckmann

Soon all the ice will be gone, and the slow transformation to spring will continue as the warmer temperatures coax the new season to life. Change like this often occurs slowly in our lives also. We wrestle with the patience of these transitions and sometimes want to hurry them along. Sometimes, it is more peaceful to let the changes emerge rather than try to rush these adjustments into being.

As Joan Anderson writes in her wonderful book, *The Second Journey*, "Nothing worthwhile can be hurried—not the seasons, not birth or death, the coming of day, the moving into night; not a composition, a thought, a work of art, or the form of a story. Patience is what makes each experience meaningful. Finding the time to be patient makes a life well lived."

What is your level of patience?

Are you normally a person who pays close attention to the steps and changes along the way, or do you rush right through to get to the next place?

Just for today, try to enjoy each moment of the day. It is amazing that you still can complete all you set out to do when you slow down and you will feel calmer and more peaceful in the process.

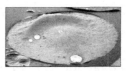

Your Droplets of Awareness...

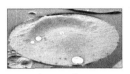

Your Droplets of Awareness...

Your Droplets of Awareness...

Change vs. Security

"Only in growth, reform and change, paradoxically enough, is true security to be found."
—*Gift from the Sea*, Anne Morrow Lindbergh

Ahhhh! It is a crisp 45 degrees as I head out onto the lake for a solo paddle in the new spring season. A beautiful morning sunrise greets me as I head across the lake into an area I fondly call the sanctuary. This sweet inlet is a refuge, a safe haven that I enter each time with great reverence.

Spring is a time of change. Everything is becoming. As I paddle across the lake, I feel winter's grip on nature releasing itself into the freshness of this new season. There is a beauty in the bareness of the landscape. What is now open and clear, will soon be concealed by summer's green. A refreshing clarity and simplicity abounds unlike any other time of year.

A doe, still partially camouflaged against the fawn colored reeds, greets me as she savors the first drink of the morning and peeks out at me under the fallen tree.

Everything is open. The stark scenery unclutters me, and I feel as exposed as the barren trees along the shoreline. Soon, new green growth will replace this unobstructed landscape. The change is imminent.

Paddlin' on, I think of so many people I love who are going through major transitions in their lives, myself included. Job changes, parental illness, relocation to unknown places, weddings, and losses of parents and siblings. Some of these changes are welcome and exciting, while others are like unwanted guests. What is staggering to me is that these changes are not minor. It seems as though we are all in a time of great transition, a part of us holding on to what was, and uncontrollable forces moving us to what will be. We are in the chasm of transformation, wondering when we will come out on the other side, and what that new scenery will look like.

Change is like the reflection of the tawny brown reeds which zig zags on the still water, even though the reeds stand still. Whether wanted or unwanted, we, too, will move in the direction we are destined to go.

Some of us embrace change and some of us abhor it, wanting things to stay the same. Some of us want security. Think of your life five years ago, 10 years ago, and 20 years ago. You are not the same person today, and thank goodness for that! Looking back, I realize that change really is security. It is the only thing we can count on. Things will change. Embracing and accepting these transitions is the key to serenity in the process. In her wonderful book, *The Gift of Change*, Marianne Williamson says, "The destination is not as important as who we are while we are walking."

Nature teaches us to be comfortable with metamorphosis. There is a security in watching the seasons change, and knowing that all will be well. With security there is freedom—freedom from harm and danger. With change there is freedom—freedom from the stale parts of our lives that need a breath of fresh air. For me, they are the same, change and security.

I watch the geese fly free, and I know that our transitions offer this liberating gift. The clarity of my paddling this morning in the splendor of the barrenness reminds me to be at peace and to trust. Change is the only security we can count on.

Williamson continues, "Can you reach within yourself for enough clarity, strength, forgiveness, serenity, love and patience? That's the spiritual meaning of every situation: not what happens *to* us, but what we *do* with what happens to us and who we decide to become because of what happens to us. The only real failure is the failure to grow from what we go through."

The lesson from nature today: Open yourself to the starkness. Gain clarity from the barren landscape. Go with the flow. Grow. Blossom. Become. Fly free.

As the gentle Irish poet John O'Donohue once wrote, "I want to live like the river flows, carried by the surprise of its own unfolding."

Contemplate a change in your life right now. How can you embrace this transition?

What can you do today, to honor and accept this change, whether chosen or not?

Move through your day calmly and allow the breath of newness to envelope you.

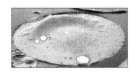

Your Droplets of Awareness...

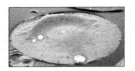

Your Droplets of Awareness...

The Shift

*"Like a rock thrown into water, the world
with its continuous changes creates ripples
in whatever is held within you."*
—The Untethered Soul, Michael A. Singer

Today is my birthday, and there is no greater gift than spending the morning on the Fox River with women cancer survivors from the Edward Cancer Center in Naperville, Illinois. This outing is very significant for me on my paddling journey. Many, many times I have gone out solo on the water to receive the healing benefits of kayaking. Often I thought of how much this experience could benefit others. Today is the chance to see if others will feel what I felt so many times on the water – peacefulness, calmness, tranquility and a slice of healing.

Although I didn't know it as we set out, this day was to be the launch of what later would become the Red Kayak Institute, our nonprofit organiz~·· established precisely for this reason.

Today's retreat offered these women an opportunity to step out of their comfort zone to feel the empowerment of paddling their own kayaks, while allowing the healing and transformative nature of the water to flow into their very being.

The day began with a light breakfast while I shared my story of kayaking and what paddling means to me. I talked about the significance of paddling in silence, because in silence we can hear what our souls need to say. The quiet allows us to open our hearts to receive the expectation of miracles. We talked about what belongs in our boat with us and what should be tossed out. Each retreater received a bag of pebbles in their kayak. When ready, one one, they tossed the pebbles into the water, 'sing anything that no longer belongs in their aka their lives. This physical releasing of ' bondage gave them permission to let go.

With that framework for our time on the water, I blessed the boats and enveloped each of the paddlers with the sweet fragrance of sage to help release any negativity. Members of the Batavia Fire Department were practicing on the boat launch and allowed me to sage them also. We all need a little release of lingering, downbeat energy.

One of my most poignant moments on the water was watching the women as they observed a Great Blue Heron on the right river bank.

I observed all heads turned to the right, watching her and then as she alighted and flew across the river all heads turned in unison to the left as she glided in front of them. This touching vision struck me, and it wasn't until I was sharing the story with my friend, Janie, and she brought home the reason why. It was a shift. An uplifting change in focus and feelings by the grace of a sacred moment in nature, which I had hoped would happen for these women today. I wondered what the message of the Great Blue Heron meant and looked it up when I got home.

When a Great Blue Heron shows up, it indicates that it is time to assert our own authority and to follow our own unique path in life, according to Shelly Szajner. That we need to listen to the inner calling of our hearts and not the ideas of others. Wasn't this part of the shift that was happening today?

We paddled on farther to an area around some lily pads that embraced us as though in a sanctuary and then journeyed back.

Our morning concluded with a group discussion, cupcakes for my birthday and a closing circle when I reminded them to be mindful of the story they tell themselves. Each retreater received a card with a series of "I am" affirmations that I received from my dear friend, Pat. "I am" is the voice of the soul. Pat lost her challenge with cancer, but left us with these affirmations which she recited every day:

I am kind.

I am smart.

I am important.

I am patient.

I am beautiful.

I am loved.

I am healthy.

I am happy.

I am healed.

I am courageous.

I am understanding.

I am strong.

I am exercising.

I am oh so grateful.

I am oh so energized.

I am oh so BLESSED!

I wished them blessings on their journey and then they in turn, blessed me in a beautiful and touching ritual. A blessing is a circle of light. The beauty of a blessing is that it opens the door to unimaginable promises. Today was the day of the new moon, which represents new possibilities.

I heard that some of the women have been out kayaking a few times since the retreat and I am grateful that they find time on the water so helpful. As one woman wrote in a thank you note, "It was a great, want to go again, pretty please with sugar on top experience." I don't think she was writing only about the cupcakes.

What are the current shifts going on in your life?

Are they adjustments you anticipated or are have they unexpectedly altered your direction?

What are you doing, right now, to recognize and embrace these changes?

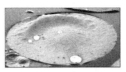

Your Droplets of Awareness...

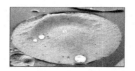

Your Droplets of Awareness...

Change vs. Transition

"Whatever word we use, our society talks a lot about change; but it seldom deals with transition. Unfortunately for us, it is the transition that blind-sides us and is often the source of our troubles."
— *Transitions: Making Sense of Life's Changes, William Bridges*

I recently finished reading a great book by William Bridges called *Transitions: Making Sense of Life's Changes.* In it, he clarifies the difference between "change" and "transition." We use those two words so interchangeably, but he highlights a big distinction. "Change," he writes, "is situational. It's a move to another city or your shift to a new job. It is the birth of your new baby or the death of your father. Transition, on the other hand, is psychological. It is not those events, but rather the inner reorientation and self-definition that you have to go through in order to incorporate any of those changes into your life."

What an *aha* moment for me! In our fast-paced world, we move from change to change without honoring the inner transition. Many ancient societies recognized the importance of this "rite of passage" and created rituals to help individuals cross this chasm from one change to the next.

As I kayaked this morning, I wondered, what comes first, change or transition? Does an external event cause internal transition, or do we start to shift inside first and then create outer change? I think both happen in different ways. Paddling in the spring, the shoreline looked barren.

Now, in August, it is lush with green – trees are in bloom and reeds are standing tall! External change in full view, but what did the leaves on the trees and the reeds go through inside to transform?

The lily pads, gracing the water with their elegance, were not visible in the spring. But now they emerge, first a rolled up tube...

...unfurling to its lush fullness, holding sparkling drops of fresh morning dew. Change or transition? Or both?

The water lily, too, emerges from its seclusion underneath, to reach towards the sun and bloom in full daylight, only to return to the deep at night. Every day a change or continual transition?

A gentle white feather floats along, separated now from its bird of flight. Did our winged friend shed this feather on purpose, or did some event cause it to lose its way? Change or transition?

Nature's transformations teach us wonderful lessons for both—by the way they allow change and transition to move along with ease and grace. It is a natural course of things that we humans can learn from.

I close with the words of Bridges who says, "After a time, each is reborn, and that is the way in which life sustains itself. It is the way of withdrawal and return. It is the way of forgetting and rediscovery. It is the way of ending and of beginning. In following it, the person crosses over from an old way of being to a new way of being and is renewed."

Today, I wish you time, courage and patience to transition. There is a beautiful new beginning waiting for you on the other side of the old ending.

Is there a new change in your life that requires transition?

What is ending, and what is beginning?

How can you carve out some time today, tomorrow, next week, to "be" in the ebb tide of transition?

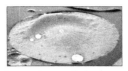

Your Droplets of Awareness...

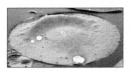

Your Droplets of Awareness...

Back Track™ and Solitude

"Look at every path closely and deliberately.
Try it as many times as you think necessary.
Then ask yourself, and yourself alone...
Does this path have a heart?
If it does, the path is good.
If it doesn't, it is of no use."
—Carlos Castaneda

My cousin Steve and his wife Diane recently gave me two very thoughtful gifts. I am very blessed for them, not only as family but for their friendship in my life.

The first gift is a very interesting navigation device called BackTrack™. It's a personal locator and digital compass. It's very simple to use. With the click of a button, you lock in the place where you are starting out on your journey. You can then mark a few places along the way that might be of interest or importance.

When you get to the turnaround of your journey, you use the places you've marked in your BackTrack™ to return to your points of interest and then eventually to where you started. Steve thought it would be great to use when kayaking unfamiliar waters or while hiking in interesting places.

The tag line on the package says, "never get lost again" and I thought about how often in our own lives we get lost, unable to find our way, unclear about our direction. Wouldn't it be great to have a device like this that could help us find our way back? Could it really be that simple?

I went to the website to check more detailed information on this product and the first thing they write about is the freedom to explore. The BackTrack™ allows me to wander about exploring and then find my way back. How cool is that? "Just pick a direction and go", it reads. "Easy to keep your bearings and provide the confidence to explore with freedom." This GPS device is designed to provide you with security while on an adventure.

As we go through our lives, through different transitions, twists and turns, getting lost is not uncommon. We think we are on one path and then something happens to alter the direction and we feel lost. We are unclear about the next steps, wondering which one is right. By being unsure, we allow fear to overtake us. And then we are stuck. So then we analyze and over analyze and don't do anything—"paralysis by analysis" they call it. And often, we never venture out to the next step.

Maybe, if we had a device like BackTrack™, we would venture out more to explore our unknown paths, knowing that we would be able to safely return. With that security, we may find that we don't want to return, but truly enjoy our new place which becomes "home." There is so much richness of spirit to be found when we risk, wander out and paddle into the unfamiliar. I think there is a device that we do not use often enough, and that brings me to their second gift.

It is a beautiful painting of a water scene with the sun barely peeking in and a solitary little boat that looks like a kayak resting on the stillness of the water. Diane told me the picture reminded her of the Solitude section of my first book, *Reflections from the Red Kayak: Thoughts on Life*. I was so deeply touched and as I gave some thought to these two gifts, I sensed a connection here.

The connection is finding our way. When I am physically out kayaking and using the BackTrack™ I can go anywhere and then easily return to my starting point. I have the freedom to wander, to stretch myself and then come back. I journey and always return a different person than when I first pushed off from shore.

On an emotional and spiritual level, I have the "device" called solitude, which is what the painting represents. In solitude, in stillness, the answers come. The thoughts, ideas and next steps emerge out of the context of my daily tasks and responsibilities. The importance of time away in stillness cannot be emphasized enough, especially in the hectic pace we swirl around in today.

I recently read a quote that said, "Solitude teaches profound lessons, especially about ourselves.

Feeling lonely has value. Sometimes we need to turn inward to discover what we need to hold on to and what we need to let go of."

Paddling solo enhances my perspective by allowing the healing and cleansing ability of solitude to flow through me. It washes out the unnecessary to allow for the new. The answers may not come all at once and may take time. But in the stillness I come to know myself better and by that "knowing" I trust the answers will come.

Henry David Thoreau said, "I would not want to die knowing I had not lived." He knew himself unlike few people do and his writing reflects the clarity of his understanding of himself. He did not have a BackTrack™, but he carved out alone time to reflect and to just "be."

And that, I think, is truly the journey. To know ourselves, understand ourselves and gain clarity about our place and our purpose on this planet. And the best way I have found is to carve out time for solitude and stillness on a regular basis. This is our BackTrack™. To never be lost again. This is our way home.

Is the life you are leading the right one for you? Or are you living someone else's vision?

Should you stay in your current circumstances, or is a different environment better for you?

How do you carve out solitude and stillness on a regular basis?

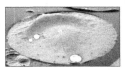

Your Droplets of Awareness...

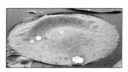
Your Droplets of Awareness...

Waves and Whitecaps

"We create patterns that others depend on,
and then the last thing we ever imagined
happens: we grow and change,
and then to stay vital we must
break the patterns we created."
— The Book of Awakening, Mark Nepo

I sit on the lakehouse porch on this humid, summer afternoon watching the noisy lake. No kayaking today—too many whitecaps on the water. The blustery, warm gale is what I call an "insane wind" blowing from the SSE between 20-30 m.p.h. Just some time for ponderin' today.

I watch the swells in the glistening afternoon sun. Like shimmering diamonds on the choppy water they move sideways, in unison, all at the same rhythm. The curls remind me of a marching band performing a half-time show during a college football game as they parade in perfect precision to the shore. The waves are swiftly moving forward with no apparent purpose except being pushed by the wind. Sparkling in a continuous pattern. I watch the whitecaps crest out in the middle of the lake, and I silently wonder where do whitecaps come from? How do these disturbances on the water get white?

I watch the waves come in, hitting the rocky shore and bouncing back, smashing into the next oncoming breaker in an explosion of suds and foam. The rebounding waves seem to be trying to push back the approaching surge, but are soon overtaken by the power and size of the incoming swell.

I am mesmerized by these waves and could watch them for hours. In and out. Cresting and retreating. Bouncing up and down. Noisy.

This scene seems to mirror my life right now. New things rushing in. Old things trying to hang on. Pushing back against this freshness. Attempting to contain the sameness. Trying to stop the adventures and forward movement with the comfort and security of the mundane. What is it resisting?

What am I resisting?

In his beautiful book, *Benedictus*, John O'Donohue frames this feeling beautifully within the stanzas from his blessing called, **For the Time of Necessary Decision**. He talks about how "time gathers its moments secrectly" and how "a force has built inside the heart that leaves us uneasy as we are."

Whatever our reasons for this unsettledness, O'Donohue describes this disconcerted inner terrain in a poignant way saying, "We drift through this gray, increasing nowhere until we stand before a threshold we know we have to cross to come alive once more."

The waves and whitecaps today uncover this deep, disquieting nudge. I continue to be captivated by the blurred threshholds of these breakers against the shore. I wonder how deeply I am going to wade into these rollers, trusting, as O'Donohue says, "that a richer life awaits us there, that we will lose nothing but what has already died." I mull over what has died within me.

Slowly the understanding emerges. What has died within me are old patterns that Mark Nepo refers to in the opening quote of this essay. Deep-rooted behavioral blueprints that define me have become timeworn. O'Donohue's words here move me as he writes, "The pale frames where we stayed confined, not realizing how such vacant endurance was bleaching our soul's desire."

My "pale frame" is replaced by an awareness of a natural spring bubbling inside just waiting to spill over like the waves crashing on the shore. A knowing deeply internal, moving me out of my "vacant endurance" to cross a new threshhold, create a new prototype and paddle towards a different shoreline of my life.

There are many questions and fewer answers. Watching the surf today, churning and moving, allowed an exciting sensation in me to surface. Change is our constant companion and with it comes a journey into the new. A chance to come alive again, to give birth to fresh ideas and to embrace the transitions and challenges along the way. I want nothing more than for my life to flow in this direction.

Bayfield, my ever loyal Labrador retriever, waits patiently for our next move into the unknown.

What newness is trying to emerge in your life? What staleness is resisting?

Is this a time for you to revisit "the pale frames where you stay confined" and let the incoming waves refresh you and give you new directions?

Is this a time of necessary decision for you?

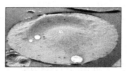

Your Droplets of Awareness...

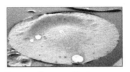

Your Droplets of Awareness...

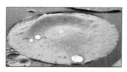

Your Droplets of Awareness...

Sometimes, We Just Go...

*"Be not afraid of growing slowly.
Be afraid only of standing still."*
—Chinese Proverb

Do you ever feel that sometimes, you just need to do something when there really doesn't seem to be any other reason than just a *knowing*? Something stirring inside, something telling you, "yes, go?" This weekend I found that when you answer that call, magical things can happen.

All week I had been wrestling with the thought of coming to Wisconsin for the Fourth of July weekend, but there were things at home that needed tending to. I could really get "caught up" if I stayed home and focused on some projects. (Do we ever really get, "caught up", seriously?) The voice pounding in my head about "The Doing" was haunting me. I then realized there was another voice calling...the softer voice of my soul, "The Being." For some reason, it was nudging me, urging me, to go. Be where I resonate, by the water. Listen. Be.

This morning's paddle across the lake into the inlet I call the sanctuary was the gift of the answer to that call. Up and on the water before sunrise, I experienced what I can only call holy. Sacred. So many times I have paddled here, but today, it reminded me of Heraclitus' quote, "You cannot step into the same river twice. Each time is different, and so are you." Today, the sanctuary was not the same, and neither was I.

As I pushed off from shore onto the calm water, I heard the trumpeting call of the sandhill cranes in the distance and the bald eagle, calling from his perch in the pine tree. As I turned to look back, I saw him alight, and fly with the freedom that only a soaring eagle can, and I gave thanks for our great gift of this country's freedom on this day.

You never know what you might experience when you enter the sanctuary, and from a distance today, it looked as though the reeds were so tall and encroaching, you could not enter. But I knew better. There is always a way no matter how blocked or closed things seem on the waterways. And in our lives.

As soon as I entered, I heard loud splashing noises coming from behind a section of the reeds. Normally, the goofy carp are noisily splashing and jumping about, but this seemed more boisterous. As I turned and glanced to the left, two deer went hopping out of the shallow water and onto the other shoreline. I smiled at their playfulness and it reminded me of what author Joan Anderson shares in her book, *A Year by the Sea*, from her conversations with her mentor Joan Erikson who says, "Joy is a duty." I don't think we allow ourselves enough fun because we are always so focused on our other duties to see joy as something essential.

Paddling farther, I went to the other side to get a closer look at some cattails and interesting reed formations. In doing so, the current turned me around and I was graced by a magnificent sunrise. Had I not decided upon closer inspection of the shoreline, this glorious opening of the day would have eluded me. It made me wonder how much we miss by not taking the time to look closer at our lives, evaluating how we are spending our time and examining how all this busyness is serving us.

Back in the middle of the sanctuary, I watched an osprey fly by and land on a bare tree branch, content to be the overseer of all that was teeming below. Watching him (or her), I became very still and stopped paddling. In the stillness came the most incredible gift of the day. Emerging from the reeds was the most beautiful young buck, meandering in the water along the shoreline. I did not move. I did not want to breathe. He was magnificent and unaware of my presence. That made me feel good as I did not want to disturb his musings. He walked in the water, head down, until he was directly across from me, maybe 50 yards. And then he slowly looked up and appeared startled to see me. Our eyes met, and we held our gaze for a few brief moments.

Looking deeply into his eyes connected me to all that is wild and untamed. His big, almond-shaped, brown eyes bore through me, as though he could see right to my very soul. Piercing. It was as though he was telling me, "THIS is right living. THIS is essential. Don't EVER forget the essence of who you are." And then, he turned, flicked his white tail and bounded out of the water into the woods.

I still couldn't breathe. I felt as though he opened my heart and poured it out for all the world to see. I sat there a long time, trembling, shaken by the feeling of everything internal being exposed in this instant. I wondered how I would put it all back and then I thought, do I? *Should* I? This indescribable moment reminded me that exposure is wonderfully freeing, whether everyone or no one is there to see it.

As I paddled around the bend, I decided to head out to one of the nearby islands, instead of going my usual way. The normal route was filled with tall lily pads and imposing reeds, and it felt too confining to go in there today. Going this new direction opened me to never before seen vistas. Through a downed tree branch I gazed at a familiar shoreline, seeing it new for the first time.

Through nature's window, I saw the reaching lily pads and the sentinel reeds in the sanctuary differently.

Very simple changes, yet reminders that we can feel refreshed by subtle shifts. Major changes often shove us in new directions, but gentle, continual adjustments can keep us on course. Help us to navigate the ins and outs and comings and goings. Help us to stay centered in the midst of chaos. Help us to be true to ourselves.

The blessings of the morning continued. As the sun rose higher, it was greeted by passing clouds, and the softness of the sky felt comforting and healing, wrapping me gently in its cozy blanket of peacefulness. Preparing me for the next set of glorious, cresting waves that will inevitably wash over my life.

Paddling back across the lake is usually challenging, being mindful of the increase of passing boats. But even the fisherman were serene today, all the boats on the water quiet. I did not feel the need to hurry across, but took my time and frequently stopped in the middle of the lake. Funny how I can feel so "grounded" on the water.

I did not want to come off the lake, but knew that soon, the speed boats and jet skis will emerge, with humans frantically scurrying about. Bringing their hectic land lives onto the water with a frenzy. But perhaps for them, that is their sense of freedom, of unabashed joy. To each his own. If they can reclaim a piece of themselves in this way, then that is what matters.

For me, this morning, I *knew* why I had come. The signs and the answers for my soul were everywhere. On this day celebrating our country's freedom, I realized that I am grateful for the freedom to experience ALL of life, to relish and cherish it. The freedom to know that in each experience, we grow, we become more of who we are, and who we are meant to be.

Today, what is your "knowing?"

Look and listen deeper. What is the gentle call of your soul's desire?

What simple step can you take today to answer that call?

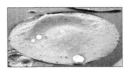

Your Droplets of Awareness...

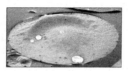

Your Droplets of Awareness...

The Voice we Give

The human voice is the organ of the soul.
Our voice is so important to our identity,
our definition and our personality
when it's there."
—Rupal Patel

I awoke today and headed out to the Saganashkee Slough for the second Red Kayak Institute retreat for the Recovery on the Water series. This is a phenomenal group of women, and we are working intensely this summer on Step 11 of the 12-Step Recovery Program—seeking to improve my conscious contact with my Higher Power through prayer and meditation.

Today is also a significant day for me as it was eight years ago that my Dad passed away. My Dad loved the woods and water, so it is no coincidence that I will be spending the morning on the water and in nature, his memory in my heart.

One of the saddest moments for me on my Dad's final journey was two days before he died. He had lapsed into a coma, and so we knew it would only be a matter of time. After spending the day with him, I left and on the way home I cried uncontrollably. Arriving, I called my aunt Stef and I shared with her what was so painful. I told her my heart was broken because I would never hear his voice again. I would never hear him say, "Be careful going home, honey," which he would tell me every time I left. It saddened me so that he no longer had a voice, and I would no longer hear it.

A few weeks ago as I was kayaking in the area across the lake I call the sanctuary, I was thinking about my Dad. This summer the theme of our retreats is "Change: Our Ever-Present Companion" and I pondered what we give voice to. So many external changes take place in our lives almost daily, but do we really give them voice? Do we really process and acknowledge the internal transitions that take place? What do we prioritize?

The lily pads are high in the water this time of year and paddling through them can be a challenge. Paddling hard makes me think of unexpected twists and turns in our lives— sometimes difficult to paddle through.

But as you can see in the picture, there are openings in the water that offer the gift of space to strategically paddle my way through. Often this is true in life—small openings of effortlessness to help us on our journey. Giving voice to both challenge and ease, we find balance along the way.

I stopped for a while to listen to the vocal chorus of nature—the chirping *con-ka-ree* of the red winged blackbird, the *twang, twang* of a bullfrog hidden in the reeds and the sound of *thump* on the water as the fish jumped. Each giving a speech in their own way to the glorious unfolding of the morning.

As I started to paddle again, I realized how hard it was to get going in all these lily pads. I thought about how we move through change and if we keep the flow going, we can paddle on our journey more easily. Stopping, and then trying to start again is harder.

Our transitions rearrange themselves. Sometimes the way is clear and sometimes it is obscure. We must trust the journey to see our way through.

Paddling back across the lake, I thought about the difference between "change," which is external, and "transition" which is internal. I found myself paddling a mantra, sort of Zen style. I'd dip my paddle in on the left and think, *"change"* and then on the right *"transition."* Paddle in on the left *"external,"* paddle in on the right, *"internal."* Paddle in on the left, *"outside"* paddle in on the right, *"inside."* Paddle in on the left, *"change thrust upon you,"* paddle in on the right, *"change you choose."* Over and over again I repeated these words in my head, but it did not feel very Zen like. In fact, it started to feel very jumbled, all this *change, transition, outside, inside.* I thought no wonder we don't give ourselves the space to move through these changes because they feel so confusing. So I decided to take a lesson from nature this morning and give voice to my mantra. So out loud to the lake I chanted with each blade of my paddle dipping into the water. I spoke it louder just to make sure the lake could hear me!

In time, I fell into a rhythm. my voice got quieter and the confusion started to dissipate. By the time I got to the shore on the other side of the lake, I was in a whisper and felt that an internal release had taken place. It felt calming like the gentle lap of water on an ever-changing shoreline.

Voice is often defined as expressing a wish, choice or feeling. Giving voice to the things that matter is important. The words we speak and the inflections in our tone are important. It makes a difference to speak our truth. When one can no longer speak, the deepest feelings of the heart are gone forever. Always remember the importance of what you give voice to.

Is there something you need to give voice to? Some change, some transition?

How will you say it, and to whom? Or to no one?

Listen today to one sound that resonates with you and reflect on what that voice means.

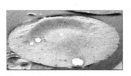

Your Droplets of Awareness...

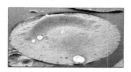

Your Droplets of Awareness...

The Residue on My Paddle

"We are constantly called upon to choose
what to preserve and what to change
in our lives. Choice often isn't easy.
But it is necessary."
—Tom Morris

I have been writing a lot this summer about change and transition. It has been the focus of the Red Kayak Institute retreats in an attempt to help our retreaters process and move through changes in their lives. It has also been a huge part of my life this year, as I shift and move in new directions.

An essential part of change and transition is letting go of the old. Often, this is the most difficult part for most of us – giving up something familiar for something unknown. Too many times, we try, whether knowingly or not, to move through to the new while holding on to a part of the old. In softball we'd say, it's like trying to steal second base with your foot still on first. In kayaking, I call it the residue on my paddle.

At first, as we are unhooking from the old, there are remnants all around, outlived parts of our lives scattered about. Is it all ours or do they belong to others? We start the process of identifying what is holding us back. We begin our way through it and it is hard to tell where our new "paddle" begins and where all the old residue ends. We try to separate, but initially it all blends together.

Slowly, our paddle raises but there are strands of the old hanging on, wanting to drag along and stay connected. Don't we all know this? How heavy does this make our paddle, carrying old stuff? Things we should let go of but somehow, we keep holding on to them. What purpose do they serve?

Eventually, we continue on our journey and work through our transition, that inner realignment that must accompany any change for it to have lasting hold. We see a scant remainder of the old. Maybe a few little remnants that still need some processing. Little bits of "something" that cling.

Finally, the last remaining piece is gone, and our paddle is clean, ready to etch the new beginning into our lives. The ripples on the water are smiling. The paddle is lighter and we are now ready for this new found freedom. We have done the work of letting go of endings, processing the transition and opening to the unlived! Keep paddlin' on...a wonderful new chapter awaits!

What residue is on your paddle?

What work do you need to do to release it?

Meditate on how good it will feel to shed these old remnants and embrace the new! See yourself as already having done it and pay attention to the lightness you experience.

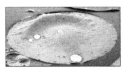

Your Droplets of Awareness...

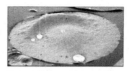

Your Droplets of Awareness...

Lessons from the Red-Winged Blackbird

The important point is this: to be able at
any moment to sacrifice what we are
for what we could become."
—Charles Du Bos

I have always been fascinated by red-winged blackbirds when I paddle through the inlets and coves on many Wisconsin lakes. How they swoop around in the marshes and then land on a tiny strand of reed. The unsuspecting reed sways back and forth, adjusting to the weight of this surprise visitor and it looks as though the bird will fall off. But somehow, it manages to hold on, announcing its arrival with a shrilling *con-ka-ree*!

The red-winged blackbird's song is considered the herald of spring, proclaiming its victory over winter. Later in the summer, they still sing their melody, but they are getting ready for their autumn transformation.

Change and transition have been the focus of this summer's reflections, and the fascinating story of this bird fits perfectly. I learned that they feed and roost in flocks, but in August they vanish. They hide in the vegetation, molt their flight feathers and eventually grow new ones. This process prepares them for their journey south for the winter.

What a fabulous lesson we can learn from these blackbirds about transition! Change, as we know, is an exterior occurrence. Some event that was either thrust upon us or one of our own choosing. Transition, on the other hand, is the internal work we need to do to get to the other side of change to the new beginning.

The blackbirds, apparently, know about transition as they gather in the vegetation to molt. They remove themselves from the day-to-day flying about the marsh, to prepare themselves for their next journey. They are content to be away for their gestation to their new self.

We, on the other hand, want to continue to flit about the marsh. Molting does not come easy for us because we want to fly from one change to the next and be okay, without shedding the old feathers. New growth struggles to take hold within us, amidst the unshed clutter.

The next time you find yourself in the midst of change and transition, think of the red-winged blackbird. Somewhere in this strand of reeds, behind what we can see…

…the red-winged blackbirds are contently molting, shedding the old and embracing the new. May you move through your transition with the same ease and trust that on the other side of the old, something beautiful and new is unfolding. A glorious beginning awaits you....the red-winged blackbird will show you the way!

What transition is at hand for you?

What one simple thing can you do right now to shed the old?

Take flight today out of the marsh, and find your space to molt!

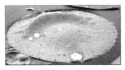

Your Droplets of Awareness...

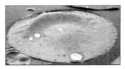

Your Droplets of Awareness...

Parting Thoughts

Some changes look negative on the surface
but you will soon realize that
space is being created in your life
for something new to emerge."
—*Eckhart Tolle*

In a small ten-foot by ten-foot area of the opening of the White Sand Creek, which branches off the Manitowish River in northern Wisconsin, I find the parting thoughts for this book on our ever-present companion, change. There is one word that resonates for me this late August morning, and that is emergence. I take my lesson from the white water lily. It is the story of a day.

Along the banks of many rivers and streams and on the shoreline of many lakes, the water lily quietly makes her presence known. Her scientific name is "Nymphaea" which comes from the Greek word "nymph." In Greek mythology, she represents feminine energy.

At first glimpse of morning light, she peers above the water line after spending her night in the deep. The light calls her to become. Among the green lily pads and strands of reeds, she peeks out, beginning her daily ritual of opening and closing. In many religious traditions, she represents resurrection, because she closes her flower at night only to open again in the daylight. She flows in rhythm with us, sleeping at night and awakening in the day. Like us, each day she emerges she is slightly different.

As the day moves along, she begins to stand taller, more self-assured and confident, embracing her unfolding from underwater bud to a blooming lotus. As the sunlight glistens upon her, she leans to the warmth. She can breathe again.

We, too, experience this change through many transitions in our lives if we are willing to trust the journey ahead. If we remain underwater, tight as a lily bud we will never be able to experience the joy that awaits or the experiences that will help us to grow and flourish. We will stay stuck, just under the surface, waiting for the right moment to emerge. I wonder, is there ever a "right moment?"

In the warmth of the sunshine, a splash of yellow appears in the middle of her flowering petals. She is willing to completely expose herself to all the elements of the day—sunshine, rain, small insects, a fierce wind or a gentle breeze and even an occasional paddler who enters her sacred space. By being willing to open, she allows herself the ability to appreciate all the sacred gifts the day has to offer.

No matter our shifts, changes or transitions. No matter how seemingly insignificant or immensely overwhelming they seem, we always have the gift of the day. Yesterday is behind us and tomorrow is not here yet. We only have now. This moment. The present. The water lily understands this. She represents peace, unity, pleasure and spiritual enlightenment. Those are the gifts of the present moment. These are the gifts that help us through the challenging transformations in our lives.

She has a softness about her. A kind gentleness emanates from her. Her purpose each day is to blossom. If you look at her long enough, a sense of tranquility comes over you. She is not in a hurry. She is not frazzled or stressed. She rests her petals on her green leafy pad, content to just be.

In the book, *A Course in Miracles Made Easy* by Alan Cohen, he says, "You thought you were here to get stuff, prove yourself, and find people to love you. Instead you are here to get peace, be yourself and find people to love. You thought you were here to fix the world. Instead you are here to appreciate what is before you and see the world through new eyes. You thought you were here to teach, while you are here to learn."

Today, the water lily is our teacher. The lessons that surface from her quiet presence are profound. The fragile water lily represents rebirth, optimism and creativity. She reminds us that we are always emerging. Always becoming. Each day in different ways. Some days, parts of us emerge and parts of us stay just under the surface. Sometimes, we keep things under the surface for a very long time, until they manifest themselves in unexpected ways. Our changes and transitions continually rearrange the innermost essence of our being.

This beautiful quote by Caroline Joy Adams encompasses my feelings on change, transition and our journey forward. She says, "Your life is a sacred journey. And it is about change, growth, discovery, movement, transformation, continuously expanding your vision of what is possible, stretching your soul, learning to see clearly and deeply, listening to your intuition, taking courageous challenges at every step along the way. You are on the path exactly where you are meant to be right now. And from here, you can only go forward, shaping your life story into a magnificent tale of triumph, of healing, of courage, of beauty, of wisdom, of power, of dignity, and of love."

My wish for you is that you may learn to live like the water lily. To blossom each day. To enter into each day with peacefulness and grace. To allow whatever needs to reveal itself to you. To manifest all your beautiful talents and gifts. To walk confidently with change. To honor your transitions. To emerge. To continue each day, to become who you were meant to be. And at the end of the day, as darkness falls, may you rest safely and peacefully in the deep, knowing that for this day, for this moment, all is well.

Each day do something for yourself. Only for you. Blossom in your own way.

Is there something beneath the surface, long buried under the water that needs to emerge? Is this holding you back from becoming?

What divine birth awaits you?

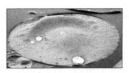

Your Droplets of Awareness...

Your Droplets of Awareness...

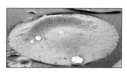

Your Droplets of Awareness...

"Water is the mirror of the soul."

—*The Hidden Messages in Water*, Masaru Emoto

About the Author

Mary Anne Smrz is an avid kayaker, who uses insights gained on the water to enrich her own life and the lives of others. She finds depth and meaning in her life from the solitude of kayaking, hiking with her yellow lab, Bayfield, and spending time in the restorative sanctuary of the natural world.

Photo by Janet Murawski

As a photojournalist and natural philosopher, Mary Anne shares her thoughts and musings while kayaking, taking others on an insightful inner journey. In her own quest for authenticity, she encourages others to find the same.

Photo by Dee Beckmann

A number of years ago, while caught in a cycle of grief, Mary Anne kayaked as much as her hectic lifestyle allowed. Paddling helped her reclaim her balance and serenity. Because of the healing benefits she experienced on the water, Mary Anne wanted to share her paddling insights with others. She wrote two books, *Reflections from the Red Kayak: Thoughts on Life* and *A Season on the Water: Reflections from the Red Kayak,* and founded the Red Kayak Institute. The RKI mission is simple: *"Encouraging people facing challenges to reclaim themselves and receive the healing benefits of kayaking. Just add water."*

She writes from her home in Wisconsin.

About Red Kayak Institute

Mary Anne Smrz and the staff of the Red Kayak Institute (RKI) ask individuals facing life challenges to leave them on the shore during their retreat time on the water. Paddling in a kayak is a perfect metaphor—the vessel doesn't have room for excess baggage, only bare essentials.

Few retreaters have kayaked previously. Many approach their first experience with hesitation, but begin to relax as they feel the rhythm of the water and the nature surrounding them. By the end of the day, most report a sense of peace, self-discovery and feeling of accomplishment.

With the help of a professional kayak outfitter and social workers from Edward Cancer Center in Naperville, Illinois, Mary Anne organized a retreat for cancer survivors in 2013. The event inspired participants so much that some women bought their own kayaks. The collaboration with Edward Cancer Center has continued for five years, with many repeat retreaters and caregivers participating as well.

RKI began a collaborative initiative in 2014 with Mother McAuley High School in Chicago, Illinois, to help raise money for the Jan Malloy Memorial Scholarship Fund. Since that time, over $12,000 has been raised for her scholarship fund, which benefits young women to continue their single-gender education. A separate retreat for McAuley Development Department staff focused on team building to advance the work of their educational institution. RKI Leadership Academy retreats in Arizona and northern Wisconsin also encouraged potential partners and individuals to assist with RKI mission expansion.

For the last four years, RKI facilitated a retreat program for women actively participating in recovery. A six-part pilot series, called *Recovery on the Water*, combined 12-Step program principles and paddling. The same women attended all sessions. Over a six-month period, they demonstrated patterns of increased self-awareness, spiritual growth and began practicing nature-based meditation in their recovery journeys.

In our fast-paced, technology-driven lives, RKI teaches the importance of "the pause." When participants get out of their comfort zone into a kayak, the simplicity of the boat and silence on the water takes them on an inward journey. Time and again participants demonstrate the value of kayaking—often in amazing ways. For example, a woman, processing grief over the loss of her father 22 years ago, cried like she had never done before. While paddling a husband and wife explored their survivor/caregiver relationship, learned about each other's cancer journey and helped each other go forward. A self-employed businessman, who lost a major account, struggled on the water because his kayak kept turning around, but then he reframed it as a message not to let a setback turn him around. He decided to release his worry and in 3 weeks, his business also "turned around."

In 2015 RKI received two grants, one from *The Friendship Fund* in Boston, Massachusetts, and another from *The Ayco Foundation*. Whole Foods also chose RKI as a charity-of-choice, to help the foundation raise funds and create public awareness. These opportunities, as well as generous donations from individuals, are helping RKI grow and will enable it to offer future retreat programs.

In 2016, a retreat for parents who have lost children was held in June at the Monee Reservoir in Illinois in collaboration with another nonprofit, the Purple Project.

The Jan Malloy Memorial Paddle, the Edward Cancer Center Paddle and the *Recovery on the Water* series have been cornerstone retreats for RKI.

Going forward, RKI is changing, too, shifting its focus to retreat opportunities in the northwoods of Wisconsin. 2018 is the inaugural launch of this new chapter for the institute.

As one retreat participant said: [To] "Slow down, enjoy the silence. Be peaceful. I was very grateful for the day."

Mary Anne echoes these feelings of gratitude—"for the opportunities RKI has received, for the people we have served and for the generosity of so many that keeps our mission moving forward and keeps us all paddlin' on."

Red Kayak Institute is a 501(c)3 nonprofit organization.

Red Kayak Institute
PO Box 98, Westmont, IL 60559
E-mail: info@redkayakinstitute.org
Website: www.redkayakinstitute.org

Bayfield Malloy Smrz
April 29, 2003-November 10, 2017

*"My instinct tells me to lie low, to process
the grief that is the partner of change."*
—A Year by the Sea, Joan Anderson,

Bayfield was born on April 29, 2003, in Wisconsin. She was a feisty, high-spirited puppy who got into lots of mischief. Aspen, my other yellow lab, was 8 when Bayfield arrived. Bayfield always liked to stand over Aspen when she was a puppy. I never understood what she was doing, but Aspen was a trooper and just let her do it.

Although Aspen was not happy about having Bayfield around at first, they became great buddies through the years.

Bayfield was originally Jan Malloy's dog and after Jan passed away, I adopted her, keeping Malloy as her middle name to retain her "Irish" heritage. Over the last 4-1/2 years, Bayfield was blessed to also have Dee Beckmann, or "Momma Dee" as her other Mom to love and care for her. Bayfield was a joyful dog whose tail was always wagging. She was always up to something—whether stealing your socks or gloves...

…pulling plastic plant containers out of the shed and ripping them to bits, taking toilet paper off the roll and "decorating" the yard or nosing her way into packages – she always made you smile.

Photo by Dee Beckmann

She loved rolling around in the grass and especially in the snow. She was always full of pure joy! Throughout her life, Bayfield had many adventures. She hiked the mountains and trails in Acadia National Park in Maine, romped around on the beaches on Cape Cod, snowshoed with us in Flagstaff–Bayfield LOVED the snow! - and got red rock dust in her paws from hiking the trails in Sedona.

Photo by Dee Beckmann

In her lifetime, Bayfield visited 28 states, her last one being Michigan, where she hiked and swam in the Sylvania Wilderness this summer. She was a great traveler – always a willing, content companion to go in the car for whatever destination awaited.

But mostly, Bayfield loved our odysseys to her home state of Wisconsin where we shared countless getaways and precious time in the woods and the waters there. She loved swimming and retrieving "Piggy" or her kong in the water. Swimming was her favorite.

Photo by Dee Beckmann

Her second favorite was hiking and we did so many trails together. As recently as a few weeks ago, she hiked a 6-mile loop on the Lumberjack Trail in the

Wisconsin northwoods and the 3-mile shoreline hike at Castle Rock Lake.

Photo by Dee Beckmann

Bayfield endured two ACL surgeries and she and I spent her recovery time together in the family room. She always was so good and accepted whatever came her way. She had so many "aunts" and "uncles" that watched over her and took care of her through the years. Bayfield was very blessed to have such great love and care. Recently, when I was in Connecticut for Dee's son Bruce's wedding, Bayfield got to share time with Mary Kay, Josette and Ann. True to form, Bayfield "participated" in the wedding when Ann adorned her with her bridal veil.

Photo by Ann Moss

Bayfield enjoyed spending time at Mary Kay's house and made herself right at home on the couch.

Photo by Mary Kay Walsh

She loved seeing my Mom, and Bayfield loved when my sister, Jan, came to stay with her and she brought her three dogs – a 16-paw pajama party! Just recently, Bayfield got to spend one last overnight with Sallie and Ken who she loved so much. I was so glad that they had a chance to share some final special time with Bayfield.

When Bayfield was a puppy, she and Josette's dog, Pita, were great buddies, grew up together and spent lots of play dates at either Camp Roslyn or Camp Wilcox. Pita died one week before Bayfield and I am sure they are running together now. Bayfield was so blessed to have so many dog and cat friends to share her journey.

Earlier this year, Dee and I thought Bayfield would not make it through the summer. She seemed to be slowing down a lot and was bothered by achiness in her hips. We took her up to the northwoods and all we said was, if this was her last summer, we wanted her to have a great one. And she did. With the help of Rovera (an anti-inflammatory that Mary Kay gave me from her dog, Cinder) and lots of swimming and hiking, Bayfield rallied and had a fabulous summer up in the northwoods. She swam almost every day and did lots of hikes and just enjoyed being in the woods and near the water, barking at the deer and chasing the geese.

We were blessed with an extended stretch of beautiful weather up there this fall and stayed on for two more weeks where Bayfield continued to flourish.

One of our fondest memories of the summer was taking her to her namesake town of Bayfield, Wisconsin. When people asked her name and we told them, they said, awe how sweet to be named for the town. We corrected them and said the town was named for Bayfield. We proudly wore the sweatshirts we bought that said "Bayfield" on them and had ice cream at the shore.

Photo by Dee Beckmann

But as things go with an older dog, you never know when their slide will begin. When we got back to Westmont, it seemed as though Bayfield's rally was over. She gave it all she had this summer and fall and she was done. Her hips seemed to bother her more, she was panting a lot, drinking a lot of water and became very restless. So the brutal decision had to be made. I always promised Bayfield I would not let her suffer and she would go with dignity. I owed that to her.

I was so blessed to be able to contact Nancy Schwartz, the vet who euthanized Aspen almost 10 years ago to again come to the house and accompany Bayfield. She is a warm, wonderful, compassionate woman, and it felt so good that she would be here with us. It felt like things came full circle.

Bayfield's last full day was a good one. We took her up to St. Francis crematorium, where we would take her the next day. We made all the arrangements and Bayfield was able to come in, see where she was going to go, and like she always did, participate in making her final arrangements. She chose an Eco friendly container for her ashes because it had trees on it – she loved the woods so much.

From there we took her to the Regional trail where Bayfield enjoyed many hikes. We strolled on the path, Bayfield enjoying the sniffs and walked her down to where the pine trees begin so she could smell them one more time. We then took her on a short path to the pond so she could dip her paws in the water one more time. She looked happy.

Photo by Dee Beckmann

After dinner that evening, she had her favorite Vanilla ice cream from Oberweiss. As I sat on her pillow with her, we recapped her life, all her friends, all she did, the places she went, what we shared. It was a great life.

Photo by Dee Beckmann

The next morning, my two little neighbor children came over with a plate of warm brownies and a drawing for Bayfield. It was the sweetest thing – a little, knock, knock, knock at the door and when I opened it they said, "We thought these would make you feel better" and handed me a plate of brownies. So sweet of my neighbor Jeralyn to do that – getting four kids ready for school in the morning and she finds time to make brownies. Amazing the love. Bayfield enjoyed a brownie along with some peanut butter and cleaned the jar like she always loved to do.

Photo by Dee Beckmann

There were so many serendipitous moments on Bayfield's last day. When I printed out a copy of the Rainbow Bridge to read to her, it was from a Companion group in Arizona. When we read our daily reading from *The Book of Awakening* by Mark Nepo, the opening quote was from St. Francis, and Bayfield was going to the St. Francis crematorium. The quote said, "You are that which you are seeking."

I went to the bagel shop to get us a little breakfast before Nancy arrived. We still had about 2 hours. On the way, I asked Jan and Aspen to please be there waiting for Bayfield on the other side of the Rainbow Bridge. At the bagel shop, there is a covered dish that sits on the counter with small chunks of bagel samples. I would always bring some back for Bayfield and today I selected the

Pumpkin bagel – a special seasonal one only available at this time of year. One thing Bayfield never lost was her healthy appetite!

When I got back home, Nancy called to say she was on her way. Dee had put her watch on at 9am earlier that morning and when she looked at the watch after Nancy called, it had stopped at 1 o'clock. Strange but we both looked at each other with a knowing glance. Dee set the watch down and when she picked it up again, it had started and stopped again at 1:09. My heart stopped. 1:09 was the time that Jan passed away. Dee reset her watch, but it never started again. Although we trusted that Jan and Aspen would be waiting for Bayfield, Jan wanted to make sure we ***KNEW*** without any doubt, that they would be there. We shuddered and we cried. These are the signs that bring you to your knees. I was so grateful to Jan and that brought us so much comfort.

I gave Bayfield one last dental mint treat – I wanted her to go with fresh breath. As we began to prepare Bayfield's place in the sunroom, it began to snow. It was the earliest day it had ever snowed here and I cried. Bayfield LOVED the snow and I let her outside one more time to enjoy the flakes. It reminded us of the scene in "It's a Wonderful Life", my favorite Christmas movie, where George Bailey is standing on the bridge and he keeps repeating, "I want to live again, I want to live again" and it starts to snow. We felt the same for Bayfield, going over the Rainbow Bridge while it was snowing and being able to live again, to swim again, to run free again.

We put on our Bayfield sweatshirts, heated the sunroom and warmed her towels to lay on. We had a sage candle burning in the paw print candle holder and had pictures of Jan and Aspen there. Nancy arrived and we got Bayfield ready. I read her the Prayer of St. Francis and we said our goodbyes. After Bayfield received the shot to calm her, she laid down her head and I cradled her in my arms and the rest of her body rested on Dee's lap. I rubbed her velvety soft ears, told her how much I loved her and thanked her for all she meant to me.

She went peacefully. She was ready to go. We had her blanket warming in the dryer to put her on in my car and we took her to St. Francis. Along with her went her Piggy and her barbell toy which was her favorite and some treats. On the way there, we had to pull over on Route 83 because a funeral was going by. How interesting we thought – we are in our own one car funeral as well. We left her lying peacefully at St. Francis. She lived 14 years, 6 months and 9 days.

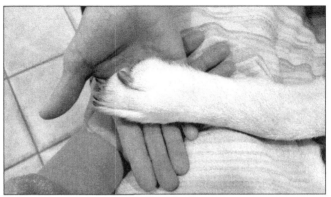

Photo by Dee Beckmann

On the way home we stopped for gas and on the little TV screen at the gas station pump, where you see messages and ads, the definition of Serendipity scrolled across. Of course it did. It was truly a serendipitous day filled with miracles.

Bayfield fully participated in every aspect of my life. It has been so fulfilling and fun to have her be a part of everything and it joined us together in immeasurable ways. She walked a journey with me that was filled with a lot of joy and a lot of grief. Through those grieving times, she both anchored me and buoyed me. It connected us in a way unlike anything I have known. She was/is a part of my soul and my heart will always be tethered to hers. The paw print of her spirit is everywhere and it is so hard to now begin my life without her by my side. There has been so much change and transition for me these last few years and my one constant has always been Bayfield. I feel unmoored without her.

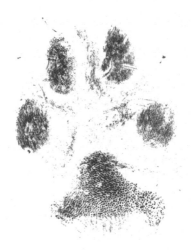

Grief is a strange companion. Although I have walked closely with grief, you never really get to know it. Each loss is different, each process of grieving is unique and the journey is never the same. Just like the saying from Heraclitus – "You can never step into the same river twice. Each time is different and so are you." Such is the same with grief.

Yesterday, I picked up her ashes and didn't know where to put them when I got home, so I set them gently on her dog pillow. I felt that was where they belonged. I put the football games on because I felt I needed noise in the house. And then shortly after I shut them off because I needed silence. But then the silence was deafening so I put the games back on. On and off all day. Restless and just didn't know what to do with myself. The house is so hauntingly empty.

This morning, in the gloom and rain, I took Bayfield's ashes out to Waterfall Glen for a Sunday morning hike. The topography of Waterfall Glen can be traced to one design maker – the Wisconsin Glacier. Maybe that's why we both loved it so much. We would often go out on hikes there on Sunday morning. I put some treats in my pocket and took her leash with me. I wanted to hike the trail along the river where she and I started this year with a hike there on New Year's Day. As I started on the trail, there was a couple starting out with their dog. Of course. On the path at the trailhead, there were some forest preserve brochures strewn about. Here is what they said:

Almost kind of looks like Bayfield on the front. I believe it was a sign from her. I put her ashes in the water by the waterfall and along the trail. After I finished that trail, I hiked another one that we did so often, putting her ashes in special spots. I hiked all the way to the end and put her ashes on some sweet little daisies that were still in bloom. It started to drizzle. Fitting. I could have hiked all day to nowhere and anywhere. I was amazed at how green the leaves were on the trees and I felt comfort in their canopy. I put some of her treats along the trail.

I crossed a bridge and thought of the Rainbow Bridge. I thought of all the love that was waiting there for Bayfield on the other side. I smiled and I cried. I put her ashes in the water here.

I passed a heart shaped group of stones on the trail and felt that it was from Bayfield. Showing me her love along the way. Back at the trailhead, I still had two treats in my pocket. I set them beside the spot where I put Bayfield's ashes when I started. It was where she and I put Aspen's ashes almost 10 years ago. One treat for each of them.

On the way home, I stopped at the bagel shop. The container that sits on the counter with the samples was empty. Of course it was. I got myself a pumpkin bagel. I felt it was fitting.

If there are some things I have learned from my previous walks with grief, I know that to continue to honor those I love who are physically gone, keeps them close to me and helps me to begin my own healing journey. I know that ritual is important and helps to create a space where signs and miracles continue to come into my life. I know that as difficult as it is, solitude and silence can be my greatest friends in grief. I know that in time, as my dear friend Nancy Cassell once told me, "Grief no longer will stop you, but it will always go with you."

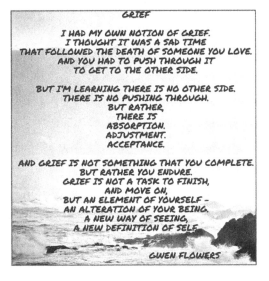

GRIEF

I HAD MY OWN NOTION OF GRIEF.
I THOUGHT IT WAS A SAD TIME
THAT FOLLOWED THE DEATH OF SOMEONE YOU LOVE.
AND YOU HAD TO PUSH THROUGH IT
TO GET TO THE OTHER SIDE.

BUT I'M LEARNING THERE IS NO OTHER SIDE.
THERE IS NO PUSHING THROUGH.
BUT RATHER,
THERE IS
ABSORPTION.
ADJUSTMENT.
ACCEPTANCE.

AND GRIEF IS NOT SOMETHING THAT YOU COMPLETE.
BUT RATHER YOU ENDURE.
GRIEF IS NOT A TASK TO FINISH,
AND MOVE ON,
BUT AN ELEMENT OF YOURSELF –
AN ALTERATION OF YOUR BEING.
A NEW WAY OF SEEING,
A NEW DEFINITION OF SELF.

GWEN FLOWERS

For now, I am stopped. Losing Bayfield is grief unimaginable and the best way I can describe how I feel is hollow. I am joyful in my fabulous memories of life with her and I am peaceful and grateful for her beautiful and serendipitous passing. But I am hollow. And I hurt. Deeply. I miss her so much. She and I always looked forward together.

Photo by Janet Murawski

Thank you for reading this long story. One of the other things I know is that writing is healing for me. And so I will continue to do that.

But most importantly, thank you for being a part of Bayfield's life. In your own way, you touched her life, and she touched yours. She loved all of you so very much, and I know, when she sees you again, her tail will be wagging....and she'll be so happy!

Bayfield gave me the gift of unconditional love. Can you think of a time when you were loved unconditionally? How did it make you feel?

Can you incorporate one act of unconditional love into your life today?

My friend, Betsy, has a beautiful phrase, "love anyway." I believe that is another way of showing unconditional love. Like Bayfield, can you "love anyway?"

Along with change, can we all make unconditional love our ever-present companion?

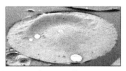

Your Droplets of Awareness...

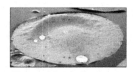

Your Droplets of Awareness

Made in the USA
Columbia, SC
26 December 2017